P R E S E N T E D

To _____

By _____

Date _____

UNCLE ARTHUR'S®

STORYTIME™

⬥· CHILDREN'S TRUE ADVENTURES ·⬥

— ❖ —

Classic Edition

Volume Three

Arthur S. Maxwell

— ❖ —

STORYGUIDE™ Section
and Exploring the Story Activities
Cheryl Woolsey Holloway

Produced by
Family Media, Inc.
Washington, D.C.

Copyright 1989 Family Media, Inc.
P.O. Box 60902, Washington, D.C. 20039

Distributed to the Trade by Wolgemuth & Hyatt, Publishers, Inc.
1749 Mallory Lane, Suite 110, Brentwood, Tennessee 37027

Printed in United States of America

94   93   92   91   90   89   10   9   8   7   6   5   4   3   2   1

Library of Congress Cataloging-in-Publication Data

Maxwell, Arthur Stanley, 1896-
   Uncle Arthur's storytime.

      Summary: Presents a collection of true stories illustrating the
values of honesty, love, faith, respect, compassion, and cooperation.
Includes activities which reinforce the lessons learned in each story.
      1. Character sketches—Juvenile literature. 2. Virtues—Juvenile
literature. 3. Children—Conduct of life. 4. Children—Religious life.
[1. Conduct of life] I. Holloway, Cheryl Woolsey, 1956-   . II. Title.
III. Title: Uncle Arthur's storytime.
BJ1631.M375 1989b   170'.83   89-23309
ISBN 1-877773-01-8 (v. 1)
ISBN 1-877773-00-X (slipcase: v. 1)

ISBN 1-877773-03-4 (v. 3)

CONTENTS

FOREWORD

Uncle Arthur's® STORYTIME™ Classic Edition has been written for every caring adult who wants to help children develop positive character traits and Christian values.

The STORYTIME program has been designed with three delightful ingredients:

a. True stories that capture a child's active interest.

b. A discussion and activity section following each story that highlights the fun of exploring the story with your child.

c. A STORYGUIDE™ section that provides helpful information on character development and positive parenting.

Although directed to parents, the STORYTIME program can be easily adapted to the curriculum of any educator or Sunday school teacher who wants to help children build the foundation of good character.

ACKNOWLEDGMENTS

Uncle Arthur's® STORYTIME™ Classic Edition is a true classic in craftsmanship. The Glatcotext Web Hi-Brite text paper provides a rich soft texture that adds distinction to the illustrations. The unmistakable typeface is Cheltenham Light. Originally designed by Bertram G. Goodhue in 1896, it was later developed by Morris Fuller Benton and cast by the American Type Foundry in 1902. Today it is one of the most widely known pure American typefaces.

———

We wish to thank the following for the many hours of professional consultation, direction, and advice in the development and formatting of this special work: H. E. Logue, M.D., president-elect of the Alabama District Branch of the American Psychiatric Association, 1989; Jade K. Carter, Ed.D., professor, University of Alabama at Birmingham, Alabama; Raymond S. Moore, Ed.D., and Dorothy N. Moore, M.A., of the Moore Foundation, Camas, Washington. And we especially thank the Moores for providing the concept of using true stories.

———

We also express appreciation and thanks to the Arthur S. Maxwell estate for their kind cooperation and coordination with the Maxwell heritage; Steven R. Schiffman for original concept contributions; Richard Coffen and Lawrence W. Ragan for providing special resources.

STORYTIME Production: Marketing and Product Director: J. Rivers; Editor: Cheryl Woolsey Hoiloway; Assistant Editor: Stuart Tyner; Project Development and Creative Director: Gail R. Hunt; Project Development Coordinator: Patricia Lance Fritz; Project Creative Assistant: Linda Anderson McDonald; Project Assistants: Suzanne A. Lukes and Vera Kotanko; Slipcase, Cover, and Book Design: Trousdell Design, Inc.; Composition: Xyvision Electronic Publishing System; Market Research: Message Factors, Inc.; Book Cover Illustration: Christy Sheets Mull; Slipcase Cover Illustration: Mark Stutzman; Illustrations: Mary Bausman, Brent P. Benger, Robert Grace, Gilbert W. H. Hung, David Lanier, Robert Lynch, Christy Sheets Mull.

AN INTRODUCTION

INDEX OF CHARACTER TRAITS

How to Use
Uncle Arthur's® STORYTIME™
Program

The STORYTIME program is a fun, easy-to-use system for positive character development. It is designed to help parents share with their children positive character traits and Christian values as they read and discuss stories and enjoy family activities together.

The STORYTIME system includes three elements:

1. Simple, true-to-life stories to share with children the traditional values and principles of good character.

2. Exploring the Story. Located at the end of the story, Exploring the Story makes each STORYTIME experience an exciting adventure. Exploring the Story helps parents and children discuss and reinforce the lessons shared in each story through Fun Footnotes, games, simple crafts, and activities designed for three age

levels—preschool, early elementary, and later elementary.

3. Each book also contains a StoryGuide™ section for parents, providing valuable information on character development and child rearing. Take time to read this section before you read the stories.

Here are some ideas that will help you personalize the StoryTime experience to fit your family's needs and maximize your family's enjoyment of the StoryTime sessions.

- Plan to use StoryTime stories as part of a routine family activity. Bedtime, family devotions, or after-school activities are a few of the times when StoryTime sessions can become a part of your family's schedule.

- Follow your children's interests. Children as young as 2 will listen to and enjoy the StoryTime stories, but if interest wanders, feel free to shorten the story or move on to other things. As often as possible, allow the children to choose the stories and activities. Let them initiate projects, and go out of your way to support these efforts at self-realization.

- Allow for plenty of repetition. Uncle Arthur's stories are easy to read over and over, and the activities are fun, but even so, you may wish for a change long before your children are ready for one. Have patience, and allow your children the opportunity to satisfy their deep interest and curiosity.

- Help your children expand their interests. Occasionally introduce new stories or activities to them. Approach these stories and activities with an attitude that shows you are anticipating adventure, and the children will soon share your sense of excitement. It won't be long before they will be enjoying a wide range of interests.

• Encourage your children to discuss the stories. Let them ask questions during STORYTIME sessions. The communication skills your family learns will enrich your family's relationship and their relationships with others.

• Refer to the convenient index of character traits found on page 8. You'll find this index useful when you want a story that illustrates a particular lesson.

Uncle Arthur® and
Character Development

Many of us, as parents and adults, wonder what happened to the "good old days" we experienced in our childhood. A time when, to us, life seemed simpler and less complicated. The family unit seemed closer and stronger. We seemed to place more value on the things we believed were truly important. Things such as the unity of the family, the basic principles of truth, honor, respect, self-discipline, faith in God, and faith in ourselves. Those invisible principles we call "character."

Today, many of us wonder if our society has forgotten the importance of these values or if we have simply forgotten how to teach them.

These questions aren't unique to our generation, but have been pondered by every generation since the beginning of time.

In 1923 British writer Arthur Maxwell recognized the need for an effective, entertaining method to teach these fundamental values to children. A method simple enough to use while they were young, when character development occurs.

Maxwell recognized that true stories—using simple examples from everyday life—are one of the most effective ways to teach children the principles of good character. He wrote, "Wrapped up somewhere in every story—every one of which is strictly true to life—is a moral lesson designed to build beautiful ideals into the structure of the children's minds."

Uncle Arthur's children's adventures have a time-less charm that appeals to the hearts of children and adults around the world. Eventually, Uncle Arthur published 48 storybooks, selling more than 42 million copies around the world.

Now, Uncle Arthur's best loved children's adventures have returned in this STORYTIME™ Classic Edition.

The STORYTIME Classic Edition has three parts which create an entertaining and effective character development program that can be used with the entire family.

- The heart of the STORYTIME program is its 30 true stories collected from around the world. Each story appeals to a child's natural curiosity and love of story time.

- Each story is followed by an Exploring the Story section brimming with activities and ideas in a think, do, and learn format that the entire family can enjoy.

- The StoryGuide™ section provides parents with valuable information on child rearing and developing positive character traits in their children.

In an era of hectic family schedules and limited time, the STORYTIME program gives parents an enjoyable way to share time with their children while enriching family relationships and teaching positive values and character traits.

This is Uncle Arthur's STORYTIME Classic Edition. Here are the stories and values that will last a lifetime. Here is the legacy of a man named Uncle Arthur.

PART TWO

THE STORIES

AND THE
EXPLORING THE STORY ACTIVITIES

Ian jumped on his new bike and dashed up the street at full speed.
Back and forth he rode, faster and faster.

There's an old saying that "haste makes waste." In our impatience to get something done, we often cause problems that make an even greater delay. I'm sure you will discover, as Ian did, that patience pays off.

Uncle Arthur

Impatient Ian

It was always hard for Ian to wait for anything. When his birthday or Christmas drew near and he thought he might receive some present he had longed for, well, he just went through great pain. Every day seemed a week, and every week a year. Over and over again he would go to Mother or Father and say, "How much longer do I have to wait?" They would remind him of the date on the calendar, but a little while later he would pop up with the same question.

It was this way when he wanted a new bicycle. Indeed, he nearly drove everybody crazy asking when he was going to get it. Father and Mother almost wished they had never promised him one, he made such a fuss.

After what seemed a lifetime to Ian, the bicycle arrived. For a moment he was contented. He admired

"I'll do it myself," Ian said. "I won't wait for him or anybody else."

its bright-red frame and shiny silver wheels. But he was impatient to ride it. So he dashed off up the street at full speed. Back and forth, back and forth, he rode, faster and faster, until he was exhausted.

The next morning he rushed downstairs before anyone else in the house was awake, eager to ride it again. Imagine his disappointment when he discovered that the front tire was soft!

Feverishly he searched for a pump, but there was none to be found.

"Where's the pump?" he called. "Where's the pump? I want the bicycle pump."

Father opened his bedroom door and stuck his head out. "What's all this noise about?" he asked.

"My front tire's soft!" cried Ian.

"Suppose it is," said Father. "That's no reason for waking the whole family at this unearthly hour."

"But I want the pump!" cried Ian. "And I want it

right away. I'm going out for a ride."

"The pump's broken," said Father.

"Then what am I going to do? I must have a pump. I want to use my bicycle."

"There is no pump," said Father sternly. "So I'm afraid you'll have to wait. Or you could walk down to the gas station and have the man there pump up your tire. And now," he added, closing the door, "let's have peace and quiet."

"Walk to the gas station!" Ian muttered to himself. "That will take me 15 minutes. Why can't I get a pump when I need one?"

There was no use fussing, for Father had disappeared, and the house was quiet again. If he wanted an early-morning ride, he would have to walk to the gas station.

Ian didn't enjoy that walk. It seemed a dreadful waste of time to be pushing his new bicycle all that way. When at last he arrived at the gas station he wasn't in a very good frame of mind.

"Hi!" he called to the attendant. "I want my tire pumped up."

"You'll have to wait a minute, son," said the man. "I have to attend to a customer first. Then I'll be with you."

Wait a minute! More waste of time. Why couldn't he leave his customer and do the job for him right away? Telling him to wait a minute indeed!

"I'll do it myself," Ian said. "I won't 'wait a minute' for him or anybody else."

Ian hurried over to the place where the air pump

was kept. He tried to attach the gauge to the valve of his front wheel.

"Better wait for me," called the attendant. "I've just had a new gauge put on, and I don't think it registers right. I won't be a minute."

"Won't be a minute!" exclaimed Ian. "You've been five minutes already. I'm not going to wait for you."

"All right," said the man, "go ahead."

So Ian squeezed the lever, and the air rushed into the tire.

"It's easy!" said Ian to himself. "Glad I didn't wait for him."

Ian was fascinated by the figures on the gauge. Quickly the pressure mounted. Twenty pounds. Thirty pounds. Forty pounds. Fifty pounds. Sixty pounds. Seventy pounds. Eighty pounds.

If he hadn't been in such a hurry, he would have felt his tire to see how hard it was. And if he had stopped to think about it, he would have known that no bicycle tire could stand much more pressure.

But Ian went on squeezing the lever. Ninety pounds. One hundred pounds. One hundred ten pounds!

Suddenly there was an explosion like a cannon shot. Ian stumbled backward, then looked at his bike. The beautiful new tire and tube had been ripped to pieces.

Poor Ian! He was furiously angry, but he didn't know whom to blame, except himself. With tears in his eyes he walked off down the street, pushing his bicycle beside him. All the way he wondered what

Father would say to him when he got home.

The attendant, who told me all about it, said that the tire was absolutely ruined. There was nothing he could have done to mend it.

"A new tire, too," he said. "Spoiled by impatience."

❖ Exploring the Story ❖

You can have a successful STORYTIME™ adventure by simply reading the story to your child. The activities below are optional additions to your adventure. Use an activity after the story is read, or save it for later. The grade levels may guide your choice, but select the activity your child will most enjoy.

Discussing the Story

Impatience has a good side and a bad side. The good side is that impatient people like to get things done. They like efficiency and speed, and they are eager to see results. The bad side is that impatient people often overlook important things in their rush to get something done.

What kinds of things do you get impatient about? What kinds of things can you do to help yourself become more patient? Describe a situation when you often get impatient. How will you handle your feelings so that the job will get done without creating problems?

Fun Footnotes

Eric Sloane, author of *Diary of an American Boy,* discovered a diary in an old house, written by Noah Blake. Noah received the diary on his fifteenth birthday in the year 1805, six years after General Washington died.

In the diary, Noah describes forging a year's supply of nails, tells how he put up a covered bridge (the floor of which Noah had to keep covered with snow in the winter), and talks about a pretty neighbor girl. Noah made his own ink out of mashed and boiled-down walnut or butternut hulls. The color was made permanent by adding vinegar and salt to the boiling water.

STORYTIME Fun Activities

Mystery Plant (preschool)

The best time to identify a plant is when it has flowers. But if you like puzzles, try picking a plant to identify while you are on a *winter* walk.

Take a picture of your plant, or draw what you find. Draw the seed pods, if there are any, and break several open, collecting the seeds in a small paper packet. Collect your drawings, pictures, and seeds in a notebook.

In the spring, see if you can sprout any of the seeds you collected. Go back to where you found the plant and see what is growing. Keep checking on the plants as they grow, so you will catch them when they are flowering.

This kind of puzzle will be a real challenge! If you still can't identify the plant after collecting all the information you can, ask your parents to help you. Or contact a teacher at a nearby school or a botanist at a nearby university or national park.

Journal/Scrapbook (early elementary)

Journals are fun to keep, and even more fun to read later on. Make or buy a scrapbook, and get a bottle of glue so you can glue in pieces of letters, tickets, menus, or other reminders of your daily experiences.

Write down the interesting things that happen to you in your scrapbook. Write down impressions of people that you meet, stories you hear, impressions you receive from new sights. Put down addresses of new friends, recipes, or new ways of doing things.

For fun, let your mom or dad or a brother or sister write down a few things in your journal. For instance, they might have interesting comments on how you looked after you took a shortcut through a muddy ditch.

Plan a Trip (later elementary)

Do you like to travel? You can enjoy visiting a new continent every year, even if you can't actually afford to go, by planning it in your mind. Pick a place you really would like to see. Write a local travel agency or the embassy for that country in

Washington, D.C., and ask for materials on the country.

Decide how you will travel to the country, and how you will travel in it. Will you go by train and sleep in hotels? Will you travel by bicycle, and camp? What parts of the country do you want to see? Find a map, and plan your route day by day.

You'll also have fun learning a little of the language. Find some books in the library that describe the people and customs. Learn some new recipes. Find pen pals (ask a library for magazines that offer lists of pen pals) who live in the country you are planning to visit.

Who knows? Someday you may actually be able to make one of the visits you have planned.

"It's the most beautiful thing I have ever owned," Emily exclaimed as she looked at the new watch.

Nothing complicates a problem more than trying to cover it up and pretend it isn't there. False stories and silence can make a mistake worse than it was to begin with, as Emily discovered.

Uncle Arthur

Emily's Sad Mistake

There was one thing that Emily could never bring herself to do. She could not admit when she had done something wrong. Instead, she would make up a story to try to cover up her mistake.

Of course, it never worked. Mother always found out. No matter how much Emily lied, Mother got the truth out of her. Emily always had to pay the penalty.

Although Emily had told dozens of stories and had been found out just as many times, she still kept on telling them, with the same sad results. One day, however, something happened that changed everything.

It was Emily's birthday. When she opened her presents, what should she find but the dearest, prettiest little watch she had ever seen! She was too happy for words. Never had she dared to hope that Mother and Dad would give her anything so beautiful.

27

Suddenly Emily noticed that her watch was still on her wrist. She leaped out of the tub and held it to her ear.

Emily put the watch on her wrist and gazed at it by the hour. To think that it was a real watch that kept proper time, and not just a cheap toy, like the ones she had owned before! How the girls at school would envy her!

Mother and Dad told her to be very careful with such an expensive gift. She was to wind it slowly, and never overwind it. She was to take it off her wrist before she washed the dishes. And of course she must take it off before she had a shower or a bath.

"If you take good care of that little watch," Dad said, "it will serve you for a long, long time."

"Oh, I'll take care of it," said Emily. "I wouldn't let any harm come to it for the world! It is the most beautiful thing I ever owned."

One evening, about a month later, Emily was taking a bath. She had done her hair and washed herself all over when she suddenly noticed that her precious watch was still on her wrist. Emily panicked and leaped out of the tub. She removed the watch and held it to her ear. It had stopped!

"Oh!" she cried. "My lovely watch! I've ruined it. I've ruined it!"

Then came the dreadful thought, *What will Mother say? What will Dad say?* She felt she could not face them. Kind and loving though they were, she thought she simply could not tell them the terrible truth about what she had done.

What could she do? If she did not wear the watch, they would wonder why. If she did wear it and they noticed it had stopped, they would question her. She decided to make up a story about it so they would never know the truth.

A number of days passed. Emily kept her secret to herself. Then one morning at breakfast, Dad asked her the time.

"I'm not sure," she said, blushing just a little. "I'm afraid my watch has stopped."

"Stopped?" said Dad. "Did you forget to wind it last night?"

"Oh, no, no," said Emily. "I wound it, all right, but—well—it just stopped."

"Let me see it," said Dad.

Emily took it off her wrist and handed it to him. "Strange," said Dad. "It looks a little misty under the glass. I wonder what could have caused that?"

"I was wondering too," said Emily. "Perhaps I got it wet when I was out in the rain last night. But I didn't

"Are you quite sure that the water in this watch is rainwater?"
asked Emily's mother.

think the rain could get through the glass."

"I wouldn't think so," said Dad. "I'll take another look at it when I get home this evening."

When Dad had gone, Mother asked to see the watch. She too noticed the mistiness under the glass.

"Very strange," she said. "I can see little drops of water in there, too. Emily, are you sure you had this watch out in the rain?"

"Oh, yes, Mother, yes. It was raining quite hard."

"No. Not last night," said Mother, getting a little suspicious. "It didn't rain at all last night."

"Then it must have been the night before," said Emily, blushing deeper still.

"Are you quite sure that the water in this watch is rainwater?" asked Mother.

"Oh, yes—er—yes—I think it must be," said Emily.

"Are you sure it is not bathwater?" asked Mother very sternly.

"No—er—yes—er—no; I'm not quite sure," said Emily, now very upset.

"Tell me the truth, Emily! Did you get into the tub with this watch on your wrist?"

Emily saw that there was no use trying to deceive Mother any longer.

"Yes," she said, "I did."

"Then why did you tell me that you went out in the rain with it on?"

"Because I was afraid of what you and Dad would say to me."

"When did you do this?"

"Last week—Monday night, I think."

"Why, that's too long ago! Oh, if only you had told me right away, instead of lying about it all this time!"

"Why?"

"Because if you had told me at once, I would have rushed the watch to the jeweler's. He would have dried it immediately, and no harm would have come to it. Now it must be all rusty inside and probably will never work again."

"Never work again!" sobbed poor Emily. "Oh, if only I had told you the truth at once! Why did I ever lie about it? Now I have lost my beautiful watch forever."

It was a hard, hard lesson that Emily learned that day. But I am glad to tell you that she did learn it. In the future, whenever she was tempted to cover up a mistake with a false story, Emily remembered what had happened to her precious watch. She decided always to tell the truth right away.

❖ Exploring the Story ❖

You can have a successful STORYTIME™ adventure by simply reading the story to your child. The activities below are optional additions to your adventure. Use an activity after the story is read, or save it for later. The grade levels may guide your choice, but select the activity your child will most enjoy.

Discussing the Story

Have you ever tried to cover up a problem, and hoped it would go away? It doesn't work very well, does it? Sometimes it even gets worse.

It's best to face up to a problem and deal with it as soon as you can. Pretend you have one of the following problems. What would you do to solve it? You can't understand your teacher in math class. You've made your family late because you can't find your shoes. You don't like where you live.

Fun Footnotes

People have tried to show the passage of time with many different devices. Long ago, ropes were knotted to keep track of time. Your mother might have a three-minute egg timer that uses sand in a glass. The sand takes about three minutes to filter through a small opening. Some games use timers like this. Sundials have been used for hundreds of years, but as one inscription on a sundial noted, "I count no hours but unclouded ones." You might remember a staircase in the Bible that was used somewhat like a sundial. Read about it in 2 Kings 20:9-11.

STORYTIME Fun Activities

"Hickory, Dickory Dock" (preschool)

You can make a play cuckoo clock to help you learn how to tell time. You will probably need your parents' help in constructing the clock. Out of heavy cardboard, cut a house-shaped clock about 12 inches high. Put two cardboard birds facing each other on the roof (use the design below if you need help making the birds), and a door flap in the eaves where the cuckoo bird pops out. (The flap should be big enough for a Brazil nut to fit through.)

Glue two different lengths of heavy yarn on the back of the clock, and slip two large beads on the bottom of the yarn for weights, knotting the yarn so the beads stay on. Draw a circle on the clock, write the numbers in the proper places, and use a paper fastener to pin on hands. You can cut durable hands out of the smooth plastic of a milk carton.

Make a mouse out of a Brazil nut by gluing on pieces of gray, brown, or black felt for ears, tail,

and a nose. Glue on two small movable eyes, and pieces of string for whiskers.

Now you have a mouse to play on your clock as you recite "Hickory, Dickory Dock." Ask your parents to find the poem for you. The clock strikes one in the poem, but you can make up verses for the rest of the numbers. For instance, you can say "The clock struck two, and the mouse ran through." Move the clock hands to two, and push the mouse through the cuckoo door.

Finding North, South, East, West (early elementary)

Find a flat piece of ground that stays in the sun all day. On the northern portion of the ground, drive a four-foot stake into the ground, straight up and down. Using a stone, mark the end of where its shadow falls. An hour or so later, again mark where the shadow falls.

Draw a line connecting your two marks for the east-west line. Your *second* mark is east, showing where the sun comes up. For your north-south line, draw a line from the stake, cutting your east-west line in half. See the next activity for more directions on telling time.

Using Your Hand to Tell Time (later elementary)

The sun moves in a 360-degree circle around you. (Actually, the sun *seems* to move around you—you are really moving around it.) The sun "moves" one degree every four minutes. Using the north-south line you found in the previous activity, line yourself up with the north-south line, facing north or south, with the sun in front of you. Remember, never look directly at the sun, for it will damage your eyes.

Stretch your arm out full length toward the sun. Now use your hand to measure the distance the sun is from the north-south line, if the line would go straight up to the path the sun travels. If your fingers are completely spread, the distance they measure is about 22 degrees. If you leave your fingers spread but fold your thumb in, the distance across all your fingers measures 15 degrees. A closed fist indicates 8 degrees, the distance between your second knuckle to the end of your fist is 3 degrees, and the distance between your two center knuckles is 2 degrees.

Once you measure the distance the sun is from the north-south line in terms of degrees, you can calculate the number of minutes the sun has yet to reach noon, or has passed noon, by multiplying the number of degrees by 4. Then subtract or add these minutes to 12:00 to find the time. This will be *local sun time,* not local standard time, which other clocks will probably read in your area. (Read up on "Time" in an encyclopedia for an explanation on how local standard time is figured.)

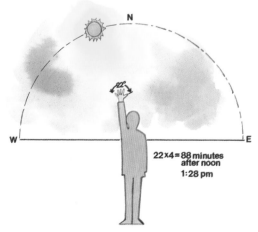

22×4=88 minutes
after noon
1:28 pm

"Joe!" cried Mother. "Leave that stove alone and don't ever play with the gas again!"

If someone were to tell you not to jump off a cliff, would you obey that rule? Of course you would. Because you know what happens to people who jump off cliffs, don't you? But what if there was a rule that you didn't understand? What if you didn't know what would happen if you broke the rule? That's what Joe had to find out.

Uncle Arthur

Why Mother Says "Don't"

Joe, don't touch that kettle!" cried Mother. "It's nearly boiling."

"I only lifted it to see how much water was inside," said Joe rather crossly. "I didn't hurt anything."

"But it isn't safe for you to touch a boiling kettle; you might get hurt."

"Oh, all right," said Joe, but he continued to stand by the stove. It wasn't long before his busy fingers were turning on the gas jets.

"Joe!" cried Mother, as she turned around from her work and saw what he was up to. "Leave that stove alone and don't ever play with the gas again."

"All right," said Joe, and he wandered off to look for something else to do. He picked up a piece of wood from beside the fireplace and began whittling at it with a carving knife that he found on the kitchen table.

Suddenly Mother noticed him again. "Joe! What are you doing now? Put that knife down. It's terribly sharp."

"All right," said Joe, putting the knife back on the table. "I'll do something else."

This time he sat down on the floor and started going through his pockets. In one of them he found a piece of wire. For a while he amused himself by bending it into various shapes. Then Joe saw the electric wall plug.

Suddenly there was a bang in the fuse box up on the kitchen wall. All the lights went out.

"Joe!" exclaimed Mother. "What have you done now?"

"Nothing," said Joe. "I was just poking this little piece of wire into this hole in the wall!"

"Joe! Haven't I told you before that you must never play with electricity? Don't ever do that again."

"All right," said Joe, mumbling to himself as he walked off into the dining room.

Mother got a stepladder and climbed up to fix the fuse. As she worked away at it, she could hear Joe saying to himself, "It's just don't, don't, don't, and then don't, don't, don't."

Mother realized she needed to explain.

When it came time for Joe to go to bed, Mother went upstairs to tuck him in and kiss him good night.

Mother said, "Do you sometimes wonder, Joe, why Mother has to say 'Don't, don't, don't'?"

"Yes," said Joe, as a curious look came into his

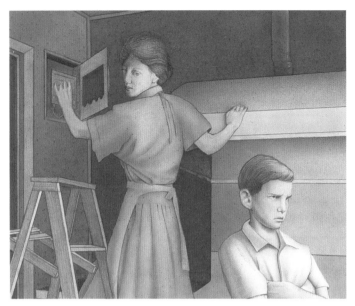

As Mother replaced the fuse, she could hear Joe saying to himself, "It's just don't, don't, don't."

eyes. How did Mother know what he had been thinking?

"Well, it's this way, honey. When I say 'Don't,' it's always for your good. Remember about the kettle this afternoon? Why did I say 'Don't touch it'? If you had tried to lift it off the stove, you would very likely have spilled the boiling water over yourself or over little brother. Then what trouble we would have had! And you would have been more sorry than anybody else, wouldn't you?"

"Of course I would," said Joe.

"If you turn on those gas jets on the stove, the gas may catch fire. You may burn something that I am cooking, or—worse still—set the house on fire. You wouldn't want that to happen."

"Oh, no," said Joe.

"Well, then," said Mother, "that's why I have to say 'Don't touch the stove.' And if you touch it, then little

39

brother will think he can touch it too."

"I see," said Joe. "But why did you tell me not to touch the knife? I was only whittling a piece of fire-wood."

"I know, dear," said Mother, "but one little slip with that big sharp knife and your hand could have been badly cut. When you whittle, use your own pen-knife, not a big dangerous knife like that."

"Well, I didn't cut myself with it," said Joe.

"I know you didn't," said Mother, "and I am very thankful. And I hardly need to tell you why you must-n't play with electricity."

"Because I blew the fuse," said Joe.

"Yes, but that's not the most important reason," said Mother. "While electricity is very useful in the right place, in the wrong place it may be very dangerous."

"What do you mean?"

"Just this, dear. What if, when you were playing with that wire, you had been standing in a pool of wa-ter? Or what if you had had one hand on some piece of metal connected with the ground? The electricity might have jumped right through you. You could have been badly burned, or possibly killed."

"I could have?" asked Joe.

"Yes," said Mother, "and I hope you see now that when I say 'Don't,' I have a good reason. I say it, not because I don't love you, but because I do."

At this Mother kissed Joe good night, and he turned over and went to sleep. The next day when Mother said "Don't" about something, Joe obeyed at once and gave her a happy little smile as if to say he understood.

❖ Exploring the Story ❖

You can have a successful STORYTIME™ adventure by simply reading the story to your child. The activities below are optional additions to your adventure. Use an activity after the story is read, or save it for later. The grade levels may guide your choice, but select the activity your child will most enjoy.

Discussing the Story

Sometimes moms and dads get busy with all the things they have to do, and forget to explain things to their children. Sometimes they forget that you are growing up and can understand things better now than when you were younger. Help your parents out by asking politely (when they are not busy) for explanations of things you'd like to know.

Fun Footnotes

Ben Franklin did many experiments with electricity. Once he tried to use electricity to kill a turkey. Something went wrong, and Franklin was knocked unconscious. When he came to, he said, "I meant to kill a turkey, and instead, I nearly killed a goose."

STORYTIME Fun Activities

Important Names and Numbers (preschool)

There are several names and numbers you need to know in case of an emergency. It's fun to practice them. Have someone pretend he doesn't know who you are. He should ask you your name. Can you say your first name as well as your last name? Can you give your house number and the name of your street? What about your telephone number?

It also is useful to know how to call an emergency number such as the police, if you need help. You can have fun decorating a card with the number on it, to put near the phone. If you have a play phone, pretend to call the emergency number, and explain a pretend problem. Remember to give your name, address, and phone number when you call the emergency number.

Fire Plan (early elementary)

Pretend you are a fireman, and check your house for fire safety precautions. You can make a fireman's hat by cutting a long rectangle out of heavy paper about 14 inches by 9 inches. Cut off the front corners in an oval shape, and lightly round off the back corners. Cut half an oval big enough for the top of your head to fit into.

As you make the rounds of your house, ask yourself these questions. Do you know where the fire extinguisher is? How do you use it? Do you know how to open the windows and remove any screens so you can get out easily? Are there stickers on the windows that indicate rooms where the very young or very old are sleeping, so firemen can give special attention to these rooms in an emergency?

Does your family have plans for exiting the house when there is a fire? Why not ask your parents to help you make a safety plan?

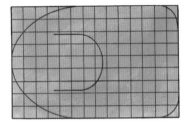

Safety Charades (later elementary)

You can make a game similar to charades that will help you remember safety rules. Write down a number of emergencies on cards. Shuffle the cards, and turn them upside down. Divide your family into two teams, and choose a leader for each team.

Each team should take a turn taking a card from the stack. The team leader should instruct each member what to do to take care of the emergency, without letting the other team know what the emergency is. The other team should try to guess what the emergency is by watching the actions of the team. After they guess, talk about what the team members did, and whether they met the emergency correctly.

Here are some of the emergencies that might appear on the cards. You are sitting in a restaurant, and you notice someone choking. What will you do? You are playing in the woods, and your friend cuts his leg on a broken bottle. He is losing a lot of blood. What will you do?

43

When Booker was a little boy, he never played.
He always had to work.

A willingness to work and to stick to a job till it's done are qualities that will take a person far in this world. This kind of steady work, combined with a love for his fellowman, made Booker T. Washington great. As you will discover, however, he did not have an easy road to travel.

Uncle Arthur

From Slavery to Fame

It is hard to realize that there were slaves in the United States not much more than 125 years ago. It's true, however, and little Booker was one of them.

Born about 1856, Booker lived in a small log cabin. There was no glass in the windows. The door was too small for the hole in which it swung on rusty hinges. The cabin had no floor but the earth. The "storecupboard" for sweet potatoes was a deep hole in the living room, covered with boards. One of the walls had a cathole about seven inches square, to let the cat pass in and out during the night. But since there were lots of other holes in the shack, Booker thought this one was unnecessary.

When Booker was a little boy, he never had time to play. He was always cleaning up, running errands, or taking water to the men in the fields. If he didn't do

Booker's mother cried and cried. "This is the day I've been praying for," she said.

things exactly right, he was slapped and beaten by those in charge.

Booker was still a small boy when Abraham Lincoln freed the slaves. He remembered going to the "Big House," as the White people's mansion was called. Booker listened as somebody read a paper to all the slaves who had gathered there. He didn't understand what it was all about, but Mother did. She kept crying and saying, "This is the day I have been praying for, but feared I would never see."

Free at last, Booker and his mother left the plantation. They walked over the mountains into West Virginia and settled in a village called Malden. But freedom did not mean a life of ease. To Booker it meant working in a salt furnace from four in the morning till late in the afternoon.

Booker did not go to school. There were no schools in West Virginia that Black boys and girls could attend. But, oh, how Booker wanted to read! He begged his mother to get him a book. Somehow, though she was very poor, she managed to buy an old, worn copy of Webster's spelling book. Little by little Booker taught himself the alphabet. After a few weeks he found himself reading that spelling book with the same enjoyment you might find in the stories of this book.

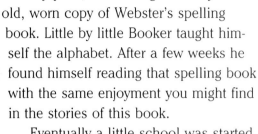

Eventually a little school was started in Malden. Booker had to work from 4:00 a.m. till 9:00 before he could leave for school. Then, after school, he worked for two more hours. But Booker was so eager to learn he didn't complain.

On the first day of school, Booker ran into an unexpected problem.

"What's your name?" the teacher asked.

"Booker," he replied.

"Booker what?" asked the teacher.

Booker was puzzled. He had only one name, so far as he knew. He had never heard of another. However, if he was supposed to have two, he would invent one. "Booker Washington," he said. He added the "T" later. (It stands for Taliaferro, a name his mother liked.)

But times got worse for Booker's family. Jobs were scarce, and wages were low. Soon Booker had to leave his beloved school and go to work in a coal mine. It was a bitter disappointment to the boy. Booker hated to work underground. It was so dark down there. Sometimes he would get lost in the many narrow passages. Sometimes there would be explosions, and people would be hurt.

Yet it was in this very mine that the idea came to him that changed his whole life. One day Booker over-

One day Booker overheard two miners talking. He crept nearer so that he could listen better.

heard two men talking about a great school for Black people in Virginia. He crept nearer so that he could listen better. The men were speaking of the Hampton Normal and Agricultural Institute. What they said sounded like heaven to Booker. He made up his mind that one day he would go there at all cost.

Two years passed. Booker had saved every penny he could for the 500-mile journey to Hampton. First he went by stagecoach. Then he begged rides in wagons. And finally he walked the last few miles. When he arrived at the Hampton Institute, the goal of all his dreams, he had exactly 50 cents in his pocket. Fifty cents to start his education! But it was one step forward.

During his long journey, Booker had slept on sidewalks and city streets. He hadn't had a bath or change of clothes for a long time. He was so untidy that the head teacher did not want to let him stay. Booker waited for the teacher's decision. Several hours passed.

At last the lady came to him and said, "The next room needs cleaning. Please sweep it."

Booker realized this was his chance. He swept that room three times. He took a cloth and dusted it four times. Every bench, table, and desk, all the woodwork around the walls, he dusted again and again till he could find not a speck more to remove. Then he reported to the lady, and she came to inspect what he had done. She looked carefully at everything, even wiping a handkerchief over the table to see if she could pick up any dirt. There was none. "I guess you will do," she said.

This "entrance examination," Booker said afterward, was the most important he took in all his life. Now he was in a real school at last! He would make the most of every precious hour that he had for study.

Some things, of course, were new and difficult for him. He was puzzled, for instance, when he found sheets on his bed. He had never seen sheets before, and he wondered what they were for. The first night he slept under both of them and the second night on top of both of them. But he soon learned what to do.

After graduating in 1875, Booker went back to his own hometown as a teacher. Not long afterward he was invited to join the faculty of the Hampton Institute, where he had been a student.

When a call came for a principal for a new training school at Tuskegee, Alabama, Booker Washington was recommended. Arriving in Tuskegee, Booker asked where the school was. "There isn't any, yet," he was told.

"Then we'll build one," he replied. Beginning with a small, leaky building, with only 30 pupils, the school expanded, until it became one of the greatest institutions of its kind in the world.

Impressed with the good work Washington was doing, many people sent him money. Andrew Carnegie gave the school $600,000! Not long after, a poor elderly Black woman, more than 70 years of age and clad in rags, came to him and said, "Mr. Washington, I ain't got no money, but I want you to take these six eggs I've been saving and put them into educating our boys and girls." Booker never was quite sure who gave the most, Carnegie or this old woman.

Today Tuskegee is a large university with a teach-

Booker T. Washington will be remembered as one of the truly great men of his time. He spent his life helping others.

ing faculty of 300 with 3,171 students, more than 160 buildings, and 5,189 acres of campus. Booker T. Washington, the slave boy who became founder and head of the Tuskegee Institute, will ever be remembered as one of the truly great men of his time. He sought nothing for himself, but worked all his life for others.

When Harvard University awarded him a degree, its president called him a wise helper and a good servant of God and country. That's praise enough for any man.

You can have a successful STORYTIME™ adventure by simply reading the story to your child. The activities below are optional additions to your adventure. Use an activity after the story is read, or save it for later. The grade levels may guide your choice, but select the activity your child will most enjoy.

Discussing the Story

Booker T. Washington had many obstacles in his way that could have kept him from being successful. On a sheet of paper or chalk board, draw a line down the middle. On one side, put all the things that made life hard for Booker Washington. On the other side, write down the ways he overcame these obstacles. For example, on one side you could write down that he didn't know how to read. How did he overcome that problem?

After you finish your two lists about Booker Washington, write two lists about yourself, or your family. What is it you want to do? What stands in your way? How can you overcome your obstacles?

Fun Footnotes

Hundreds of years ago people drew huge pictures on the ground by cutting away topsoil and letting the lighter undersoil show. A design that looks like a chalk-white horse cut into the soil in Uffington, England, seems to gallop across the field. A huge man and a four-legged, long-tailed animal have been scraped into the desert sand near Blythe, California. No one knows for sure why these pictures were made or who made them.

STORYTIME Fun Activities

Making Giants (preschool)

To make a giant, you need a large, relatively even surface like a parking lot or an evenly sloping hill. A hill would be the best choice, because then you can stand at the bottom and see what you have made.

Decide what kind of giant you want to create. Do you want a giant person or animal, or do you want to design a huge truck or ship? Next, decide what materials you need to make your giant. You can use rope, rocks, loose boards, or anything else that can be lined up. Big chunks of carpenter's chalk can be used to mark pavement. (Have an adult help you, and be sure you have permission to mark on a parking lot.)

Use your materials to make an outline of your giant. Fill in some details in your giant, too. A whale could use an eye and a blow hole. A truck needs wheels and a cab. Now you and your giant are ready to play!

A Dinosaur in Your Room (early elementary)

Try using a toy dinosaur to throw a shadow on your bedroom wall. You can put up newspapers (where the shadow falls). Use putty sold for the purpose of hanging posters. Mark the edge of the shadow, and  cut away the rest of the paper so a paper outline of your giant pet remains. Add more features if you want to, such as a long neck or fins for a dinosaur. Paint or glue on crepe paper scales.

You can make a friendly beast encircle your room, or look down at you from the ceiling. And don't forget to give him a name!

Constellations (later elementary)

Something about looking at the stars puts our own importance in proper perspective. Theodore Roosevelt had a ritual he followed before he went to bed. He would find a patch of light near the constellation Pegasus. "That is the Spiral Galaxy in Andromeda," he would say. "It's as large as our Milky Way. It is one of hundreds of millions of galaxies. It consists of 100 billion suns, each larger than our sun." When he felt small enough, he would go to bed!

You can make a device to practice identifying constellations. Use a round oatmeal box, black construction paper, and a flashlight. Cut the center out of the lid of the oatmeal box, leaving about an inch of rim. Punch holes for each constellation you want to learn in a circle of black paper, cut to fit inside the lid of the oatmeal box. Put the lid on the box, and shine the flashlight inside the box, throwing the pinpoints of light showing the constellation on the ceiling or wall.

Big Dipper

Little
Dipper

I could be the happiest girl in the world, *thought Debbie.*

Luck and circumstances might get someone a dollhouse once in a great while, but not nearly as often as hard work does. At least, that's what Debbie discovered. Whatever it is your heart desires, see if Debbie's method might work for you.

Uncle Arthur

How Debbie Got Her Dollhouse

For a very long time, it seemed years and years, Debbie had wanted a dollhouse. Whenever she saw one in a store she would stare at it just as long as Mother would let her stand at the window. She thought that if only she could have a dollhouse all her very own, she would be the happiest girl in the world.

Over and over again Debbie had come to Daddy and said, "Daddy, please get me a dollhouse for my birthday." Or "Daddy, please get me a dollhouse for Christmas."

Every time Daddy had replied, "I'm sorry, Debbie, but they are far too expensive. As much as I would like to, I just couldn't manage to buy you one."

Debbie would go on hoping and hoping that someday, maybe, she would be able to buy one herself. The only trouble about that, however, was that Debbie never seemed to be able to keep her money. If she was given a dime, she would spend it right away for candy. If she was given a quarter, she'd run to the store and buy some little things she had seen. She had nothing saved up for anything so expensive as a dollhouse.

One day Debbie came running home from school greatly excited.

"Daddy!" she cried. "Daddy! There's a girl at school who has a dollhouse, and she wants to sell it. May I buy it?"

"Of course," said Daddy, "if you have enough money."

"I don't have any money," said Debbie. "At least, I don't have any except that dime you gave me yesterday. I haven't spent that yet."

"How much does the girl want for her dollhouse?" asked Daddy.

"Only $20," said Debbie. "And she says that that is very cheap, because it includes all the doll furniture and things."

"Twenty dollars!" exclaimed Daddy. "That is a good price. But it's a lot of money when you have only a dime, isn't it?"

"I'm afraid it is," said Debbie.

"Do you know how many dimes there are in $20?" asked Daddy.

"No," said Debbie. "I never added them up."

"Well, there are 200," said Daddy.

"Oh!" whistled Debbie. "That's a lot of dimes. But, Daddy, what if I were to save up 200 dimes—"

"That's a great idea," said Daddy with a twinkle in his eye. "Do you really think you can do it?"

"Daddy, I never wanted anything before like I want this dollhouse."

*"I'm going to save all my money from now on," said Debbie,
"until I have 200 dimes."*

"If you really want to save the money," said Daddy, "you will have to be very serious about it. You'll have to stop buying candy and trinkets."

Debbie blushed a little at this, but she was really determined now.

"Look, Daddy," she said, "I'm going to save all my money from now on. And when I have 200 dimes, I'll buy that dollhouse."

"That's my girl," said Daddy. "I'll tell you what I'm going to do. When you have saved 10 dimes I'll give you 10 more to add to your savings. We'll work together until you have your dollhouse."

"Will you, Daddy?" cried Debbie, jumping about in glee. "Now I'll be able to buy my dollhouse."

"I'm sure you will," smiled Daddy. "But, remember, be patient. You do have quite a long way to go. By the way, how do you propose to earn all this money?"

"I'm going over right now to ask Mrs. Brown if she'd like her back porch painted. Then I'll ask Mr. Morgan about raking the leaves in his yard. Then I'll—"

"Now you're talking good sense," said Daddy. "That's fine. Maybe I could find you a few jobs too, if you want them."

"I do," said Debbie. "Oh, Daddy, I can almost see the dollhouse sitting in my bedroom now!"

Debbie started on her great new plan. Instead of wasting her spare minutes, she turned them into money, dime by dime. It was hard work, of course, but every good thing costs something.

When her friends would come to ask her to play at their house or go to the park, she would say, "Sorry, but I have a job to do." It was dreadfully hard to see them go off without her. But just as she felt tempted to quit her work and follow them, she would think of her dollhouse and stay by her job.

Debbie stopped spending her money on little things, too. Instead she would take her precious dimes and put them in her bank. Of course, every time she had 10 dimes in it, she would call on Daddy for his 10.

Daddy seemed to be paying out 10 dimes every week

There were tears in Debbie's eyes and on her cheeks.
"That girl's mean for selling it," she said.

or two. He was glad, however, for he could see that
Debbie was learning lessons of priceless value.
Months passed by, and the precious bank became
heavier and heavier.

But then one day something tragic happened. It
was the very day before Debbie's birthday. She came
home from school brokenhearted. There were tears in
her eyes and some on her cheeks and a lot more on
her dress.

"What's the matter?" asked Daddy.

"That girl sold her dollhouse," said Debbie, breaking down. "And now I can't have one after all."

"Oh no, Debbie," said Daddy. "That's too bad. After all your hard work, too."

"Imagine her selling it just when I was ready to
buy it from her!" said Debbie.

"Well," said Daddy, "now you will be able to use
your money for something else. There'll be lots of

Debbie's face was beaming with joy.
"How did it get here?" she asked.

other things you'll want later on."

"I don't want anything else but my dollhouse," said Debbie. "It's a shame. She's mean for selling it."

"Don't take it so hard," said Daddy. "Let's go for a walk together and try to forget all about it."

"A walk!" exclaimed Debbie. "I don't want to go for a walk. And besides, I'll never forget about it as long as I live!"

"Oh, just a little walk upstairs," said Daddy, smiling.

"Upstairs?" asked Debbie, curious at once. "Why upstairs?"

"Oh, just for a little walk," said Daddy, leading the way.

Very much puzzled, Debbie followed Daddy upstairs. Mother came along too. As Debbie entered her bedroom, her tear-stained face suddenly lit up with surprise and joy. There on the floor was the very dollhouse she had wanted so long and worked so hard to buy.

"Why, it's my dollhouse!" she exclaimed. "How did it get here?" Debbie's face was beaming with joy.

"Oh, it just came," said Daddy.

"No," said Debbie. "It couldn't have just come by itself."

"You're right," said Mother. "Daddy bought it from that girl weeks ago. When we saw the way you were working for it, we thought it would be too bad to have her get tired of waiting and sell it to somebody else. So here it is. And you deserve it. Daddy and I love to see our girl work so hard and save so much as you have."

"Hurrah!" yelled Debbie, twirling around the room in glee. "Oh, say, Mother and Daddy, if you'd like to come and play with this dollhouse anytime, you may, you know."

"Thanks for the invitation," said Daddy, and together they sat down on the floor and began arranging the doll furniture in all the rooms of Debbie's dollhouse.

You can have a successful STORYTIME™ adventure by simply reading the story to your child. The activities below are optional additions to your adventure. Use an activity after the story is read, or save it for later. The grade levels may guide your choice, but select the activity your child will most enjoy.

Discussing the Story

Money is useful, but it takes practice and patience to get the most benefit out of it. Do you have any plans for saving money? Do you have a place where you can save money? Why not ask a nearby bank how to start a savings account? Find out the minimum amount you can deposit. Once you have a savings account, get in the habit of adding to your account every month, even if it is just a small amount.

Fun Footnotes

People through the ages have developed many kinds of money. Money can be anything that is accepted as an appropriate exchange for valuable goods or work. Yap islanders use huge flat stones with a

hole in the center for money. They display them in front of their houses.

Ancient Chinese made money in the form of bronze spades and knives. Natives of the Santa Cruz Islands, northeast of Australia, glued bird feathers on a rope coil to use for money. Roman soldiers used to be paid in salt, which led to the saying "He's not worth his salt," describing a person whose work wasn't worth his wages.

STORYTIME Fun Activities

A Fistful of Pennies (preschool)

Have you ever had trouble holding on to money? Coins are fun to hold, but they are easy to drop and lose, aren't they? Where is the best place to keep your money? This finger play will give you a hint. You will need five pennies. Drop the pennies in your hand as you count them in the finger play, and drop each one in your lap as it gets "lost." If you have a bank, use it for the last penny. Shake your bank when you finish saying the poem.

One penny, two pennies, three, four, five.
One penny dropped under uncle's beehive.
One penny, two pennies, three pennies, four;
One penny rolled out under a door.
One penny, two pennies, three pennies still;
One penny's lost in the grass on the hill.
One penny, two pennies here with me yet;
But I have a hole in my pants pocket.
One penny now, but I'll put it away—
Safe in my bank for some other day.
When I get more pennies, I know what to do.
I'll put *them* safely in my bank, too!

—Cheryl Woolsey Holloway

Keeping Track of Your Allowance (early elementary)

Do you feel you need more allowance than your parents feel you need? Maybe you don't get any allowance at all. Since learning how to keep track of money is such a useful experience, perhaps you can persuade your parents to increase your money responsibilities.

For several weeks, keep track of every penny you receive as allowance or otherwise. Keep a notebook just for this purpose, and write down what you receive, and what you spend it on. Keep a receipt of every purchase.

When you are satisfied that you can keep track of your money, plan a budget for a week. (You can plan a budget even if you receive no allowance.) Plan what you will need for lunches, school supplies, and recreation, and be sure you are being realistic in your needs.

Show your record keeping to your parents, as well as the budget you have planned for one week. Ask them to increase your allowance to meet your budget, if they think your budget is reasonable. Promise to show them your bookkeeping records at the end of every week. You can make a deal that every penny that is unaccounted for can be deducted from your next allowance. See what your parents think about this idea. You might be surprised!

JAMIE'S
WEEKLY BUDGET
LUNCH ----- $ 5.00
FUN 6.00
CLOTHES 4.00
GIFTS 2.00
SUPPLIES 3.50
MISC. 1.75
TOTAL $ 22.25

Making Investments (later elementary)

How much money do you have right now? Why not give yourself a challenge? See if you can double the money you have in two to four weeks. You will have to plan how you can do this. What can you buy with the money you have that will make more money?

You may be able to rent a piece of equipment to do a job, such as a lawn mower, or window-cleaning equipment. You may be able to purchase some raw materials such as cloth, leather, or paper and ink, and make something to sell. You may use your funds to advertise a service you can provide, such as lawn mowing, or baby-sitting.

You can also invest other things besides money. The time you spend studying is an investment in your future. You expect to receive some profit later on from the effort you spend on your studies now. The efforts you spend in making wise friendships, learning to use your time, learning how to look at and remember people, colors, shapes, and events around you—these are investments, too. Every honest effort in developing your skills pays off, though not always in money.

"If I'm not the unluckiest fellow who ever lived," Jim said to himself as he gazed into the window.

How would you feel if someone teased you unmercifully because you had done something nice for someone else? You might feel unlucky, just like Jim. But Jim's good deed gave him such joy that I don't think you would have minded being in his shoes at all.

Uncle Arthur

Unlucky Jim

Jim thought he was the most unlucky boy who had ever been born. Everything seemed to go wrong. Life looked particularly dark to him just now. Only a few minutes ago his one and only glass marble had rolled down a drain.

Actually Jim had quite a bit to make him feel unhappy. For one thing, he was shivering with cold. He should have had warm socks and underclothes to wear. But he didn't have any because there was not enough money to buy them. Father was out of work.

For another thing, he was hungry. It had been several hours since lunch. The bit of bread and vegetables he'd had then seemed to have gone clear down to the South Pole. Jim trudged along the streets with his hands in his pockets. He saw lots of other boys and girls walking into beautiful homes for their supper. He knew that he would have to climb up the narrow stairs of a crowded apartment for the little bit of bread he'd get for his supper.

Just then Jim passed a toy shop ablaze with lights and full of everything that might make a boy's heart glad. He stopped a moment and watched other boys and girls coming out of the store with packages under their arms. He jabbed his hand a little deeper down into his pocket and fingered a nickel, his very last coin. How he wished that he could buy something to take to his little sister, Jean! She was sick, lying in her bed at home. If he could only get something she would really like.

"If I'm not the unluckiest fellow that ever lived!" Jim said to himself.

The next day, however, his luck changed. He was walking down the street when a well-dressed woman stopped and spoke to him.

"Is your name Jim Mackay?" she asked.

"Yes, ma'am," said Jim, surprised, and wondering what was going to happen.

"Well," said the woman, "we have your name on a list at our church. We want you to come to a special Christmas party next week. Here is a ticket for you."

"Oh!" said Jim, not knowing what else to say. "But what about Jean, my sister? She's sick today, but I'm sure she'll be better by then. Can she come too?"

"I'm afraid we can take only one from each family this time," said the woman kindly. "We will try to take Jean next time."

As Jim approached the gift-laden tree a new idea entered his mind.

"Well, that's lucky and unlucky," said Jim to himself as the woman walked away. "Lucky for me and unlucky for poor Jean."

And then a bright idea occurred to him. Perhaps he could let Jean go instead of him. He looked at his card. It read "Admit bearer—Jim Mackay."

"Unlucky again!" thought Jim.

So Jim went to the party. For most of the time, he forgot all about his troubles. Everything was so different, so wonderful. He had never, never had so many good things to eat.

After the meal they all played games until it was time for the Christmas presents to be given away. What excitement there was then, especially as each child was to be allowed to choose just what he wanted most.

Jim could hardly sit still as he watched the other children going up to the tree. He felt as if he were on pins and needles. He had seen such a wonderful toy fire truck hanging on the tree—something he had wanted all his life. How he did hope and hope and hope that no one else would ask for it first!

At last, after what seemed hours, Jim's turn came to make his choice.

"Jim Mackay!" called out the woman by the tree.

Jim jumped from his seat like a shell from a cannon. All he could see was the red fire truck. It was still there!

As he approached the woman, he noticed that she was the very one who had given him his ticket for the party. Immediately a new idea entered his mind.

"And what would you like to have, Jim?" asked the woman. "You may have any one thing you like from the tree."

What an offer! Jim could scarcely take it in. He stood and gazed up at the sparkling tree. Once more his eye caught sight of the fire truck.

"I'd really like that red fire truck," he said, looking up at the lady. "But if you don't mind, I'll take that doll over there."

Tears filled his eyes as he said it, but with great determination he kept his face straight ahead.

Somehow the woman seemed to understand, and without a word she gave Jim the doll. As he went away she squeezed his hand. Bending down, she whispered, "God bless you, Jim."

But the other children did not understand at all. They giggled and snickered, whooped and yelled as they told everyone that Jim had chosen a doll! Some of the boys called out, "Sissy!" and others

ADMIT BEARER
ONLY
Jimmy McKay.

Jim danced a jig around Jean's bed, laughing and hugging the red fire truck.

said with a laugh, "Imagine a boy taking a doll!"

The little girls said, "That was just the doll we wanted!"

Jim blushed. He couldn't help it. Finally he became so uncomfortable that he put on his cap and went out, with the doll under his arm.

All the way home he thought about the bad luck that seemed to have followed him. First he had lost his fire truck. Then he had been laughed at by the whole crowd of children.

"If I'm not the unluckiest fellow—" he began. Then he felt the doll under his arm. At once his thoughts brightened and his step quickened.

A few minutes later he was up in the little dark bedroom where Jean lay sick in bed.

"I'm so glad you've come!" said Jean. "It's lonely here. What have you got there?" she asked, sitting up in bed and peering at the doll with eager eyes. "Is that

73

for me? Oh, Jim, you're so kind!"

Jim forgot all about his bad luck. A thrill of joy went through him as he saw his sister's delight.

Just then there was a knock at the door. It was the woman from the church. "What—?" began Jim.

"I've come to say how sorry I am that the children were so unkind to you this evening," said the woman. "They are sorry too, now. I told them why you chose the doll. They asked me to bring you something for yourself. Here it is. Now I must go, for it is getting late. Good night!" And she was gone.

Jim gasped, and opened the package. What do you suppose he found? It was the fire truck! Jim jumped up and down all around Jean's bed. Then he chuckled to himself and said, "If I'm not the luckiest fellow alive!"

❧ Exploring the Story ❧

You can have a successful STORYTIME™ adventure by simply reading the story to your child. The activities below are optional additions to your adventure. Use an activity after the story is read, or save it for later. The grade levels may guide your choice, but select the activity your child will most enjoy.

Discussing the Story

Jim's habit of thinking about how to make his sister happy wasn't an accident. You too can be as thoughtful as Jim was. Use some of these ideas to help you.

Start when you wake up. Try thinking of something you can do to make someone else happy today. If you say a prayer first thing in the morning, try praying about others first, before getting around to yourself.

Try going through a whole day, making everyone else around you as happy as you can. At the end of the day go over what happened, and see how *you* feel. Was it a good day for you too?

Fun Footnotes

Long ago the Norse and Anglo-Saxons burned a huge oak log. They called it "Juul" (pronounced **yool**). Eventually the burning of the Yule log became part of Christmas celebrations. The word for Christmas in Lithuania means "log evening."

The English also burned the Yule log, and thought it was good luck to save a piece of the unburned log to burn with the next year's log. The Serbs in Yugoslavia think it's bad luck if the log burns out, and keep someone watching all night to make sure that doesn't happen!

STORYTIME Fun Activities

Making a Six-point Star (preschool)

The star is a symbol of Christmas that is used all over the world to represent the star that the Wise Men followed to find Baby Jesus. Stars made out of light wooden frames covered with tissue paper, tinsel, and tassels decorate many homes in the Philippines at Christmastime.

You can make a star out of wire coat hangers. Choose six hangers the same size, with straight sides. Lay three hangers on a flat surface, hooks pointed inside, using the bottoms of the hangers to form a triangle. The three hooks will overlap each other in the center of the triangle. Make another triangle with the other three coat hangers, and lay this triangle on top of the first triangle, forming a six-point star. Using thin wire or string, fasten the coat hangers securely together at each corner, and at the center.

To decorate your star, you can tie bows on the six

points of the star, and use a large bow to cover the hooks at the center of the star. Or you can cover the star with tissue paper, crepe paper, or fabric glued to the wires. Make tassels out of tinsel, yarn, or strips of tissue paper, and tie a tassel to each point of the star. You can hang your Christmas star on a porch, on a door, or over your dining room table.

The Piñata (early elementary)

In Latin America, Posada comes before Christmas and lasts nine days. Each night of Posada, children carry figures of Mary and Joseph through the house, stopping at each door and begging to enter. When they reach the room containing the stable, they put the figures inside. On Christmas Eve they put a figure of Baby Jesus in the manger. After this enactment come fun and games, and the children help break a piñata (pronounced **peen YAH tuh**), a hanging container filled with goodies.

You can make a piñata with papier-mâché. Soak newspaper strips in water. Make a paste out of flour and water, dip the wet newspaper into this paste, and plaster several layers around a balloon you have blown up. Don't put on too many layers, or the piñata will be hard to break.

Use toilet paper tubes for legs, and a smaller blown-up balloon to give shape to the head. Attach legs and head with papier-mâché strips, and allow to dry. Cut a hole in the top of your creation, and remove the balloon. Decorate your piñata with paint or fringed crepe paper, and fill it with small items such as nuts, balloons, stickers, and candy. Hang the piñata so even the smallest members of your family can take a turn at breaking it.

The Nativity Scene (later elementary)

Setting up a Nativity scene is an important part of Christmas for many people. Italians have a special ceremony around their miniature scene of Bethlehem while the mother places a figure of the Bambino (Baby Jesus) in His manger bed.

One way of making your own Nativity scene is to use ¾-inch dowels, small painted wooden heads (found in a craft shop or molded out of dough), pipe cleaners, and scraps of material. Cut the dowels into 2- or 2½-inch lengths. Round off one end of each dowel for shoulders, and glue on a head. Fold back each end of a 2-inch length of pipe cleaner for hands, and glue the middle of the pipe cleaner at the back of the head and shoulders.

Dress each figure appropriately. A small rectangle of material folded over each arm and glued together at the bottom makes sleeves. Choose heavier, contrasting material for a cloak. To make one, split a rectangle of material 4 to 5 inches long by 1½ inches wide to the center, where you should cut out a small circle for the neck. (See illustration.) The opening can go in the front or in the back. Use silks and rich colors for the Wise Men, decorating them with sequins and plastic jewels. Fashion turbans for the Wise Men's heads, and glue gold braid down the front of their robes.

Bombs were falling everywhere. People rushed into shelters for safety.

Thinking of others is a sure cure for the blues, as Garry learned from a boy in circumstances much worse than his.

Uncle Arthur

Thinking of Others

Garry was wandering around the house looking as though he had a tooth-ache, toeache, and tummyache all at once. Nothing was right. He had never in all his life felt so blue.

"What is the matter with you, Garry?" asked Mother. "What's making you so miserable?"

"Oh, everything's the matter," growled Garry.

"Well, what?"

"Oh, I'm just fed up."

"What about?"

"Oh, my friends are so mean. They're always teasing me and criticizing me. They don't want me to play with them, and they always leave me out if they can. I hate having anything to do with them."

"Are you sure it isn't your fault?"

"My fault! Of course it isn't," said Garry fiercely. "How could it be my fault?"

Garry was miserable. He was acting as though he had a toothache, toeache, and tummyache all at once.

"Oh, I just wondered," said Mother. "Sometimes even the best of us make mistakes."

"What do you mean?" grunted Garry. "How have I made a mistake?"

"Well," said Mother cautiously, "I was just wondering whether you had been as kind to them as you want them to be to you."

"Of course I'm friendly."

"Are you sure?" asked Mother. "Do you really go out of your way to show your friends you like them? Do you try to take an interest in what they want to do? Or do you always expect them to follow your suggestions and please you?"

"I dunno," muttered Garry.

"Could it be that the real reason you are miserable is that you are thinking about yourself?" asked Mother. "You have let yourself get upset because the other boys have said or done something that hasn't pleased you. If you start planning how to do something kind for them—"

"Something kind for them?" cried Garry.

"I mean it," said Mother. "The best cure I know for the blues is to start thinking of others. Just forget how you've been hurt and begin working out a plan to help somebody else who is having a hard time. Think of some kind, encouraging thing to do."

"That's all right to talk about, but I couldn't encourage anybody," growled Garry rather rebelliously.

"I don't believe you could just at present," said Mother, smiling. "But let me tell you a story."

"What's it about?"

"It's about the blitz," said Mother.

"What about the blitz?" asked Garry, a glint of interest coming into his discouraged face.

"I'll tell you," said Mother. "It was one of the worst days of World War II. Hundreds of enemy planes were over London, and bombs seemed to be falling everywhere. A lot of people rushed for safety into a shelter.

"About 250 people were in the shelter, all lying on the floor and praying that the next bomb wouldn't hit them. Among the crowd, quite unrecognized, was a minister of a large church. He was lying on the floor too, with all the rest. Like everybody else, he was very uncomfortable and very much afraid.

"The noise was deafening. This was not one of the deep, underground shelters. It was just a building on the surface. The roar of antiaircraft guns and the crash of exploding bombs made everybody nervous.

"The minister pulled a book out of his pocket and tried to read, but he couldn't. There was too much disturbance. Just then a small voice spoke to him. The minister turned. There beside him was a young lad,

"Wouldn't you get to sleep better if I was to take off your boots?" said the little boy.

quite calm among the fury of the battle raging all around.

"'Say, mister,' said the little boy, 'wouldn't you get to sleep better if I was to take off your boots?' That was all he said, but how much it meant at such a time! The minister, I know, will never forget it. Just think of it, Garry! All the people in that shelter were so worried and anxious, wondering whether they would ever get out alive. But that one dear little lad was thinking of their comfort, and how he could help them get to sleep."

"He sure was brave," said Garry.

"He was," said Mother. "And not only brave, but wise. For while he was thinking how to be kind to others he forgot about himself. He wasn't afraid and he didn't get upset, despite all the disturbance."

"I see what you mean," said Garry.

"I'm glad you do," said Mother. "It makes such a

difference when we understand this great secret: thinking of others rather than of ourselves brings true happiness."

❖ Exploring the Story ❖

You can have a successful STORYTIME™ adventure by simply reading the story to your child. The activities below are optional additions to your adventure. Use an activity after the story is read, or save it for later. The grade levels may guide your choice, but select the activity your child will most enjoy.

Discussing the Story

Thinking of others can help you ignore the hurts and troubles you have. Make a list of things you can do to help you adjust to disappointment, someone else's bad treatment of you, or a difficult change in your life. Use the following ideas to help you get your list started.

Make a new friend.

Learn about the needs of a new pet.

Plant a flower garden so you can have flowers to give away.

With your parents, get to know some old neighbors better.

Fun Footnotes

Thinking of others can help you do things you wouldn't be able to do otherwise. Many brave feats have been performed because of others' needs, though the hero wasn't brave enough to stand up for himself.

Clara Barton was a courageous nurse on the battle-fields of the Civil War. Her first appearance on the battlefield was at Antietam, the bloodiest day in the history of the United States. She came close to death many times while she helped care for the wounded and dying. Yet, as a girl, she was very shy, unable to go to school with girls her own age.

When you think of others, you might be surprised at what you can do.

StoryTime Fun Activities

Count Your Friends (preschool)

How many friends do you have? Can you count them all? You can make a caterpillar to help you see how many friends you have. Cut plenty of paper cir-

cles about 1½ inches in diameter. Make them many different colors. For the caterpillar's head, use a little larger circle with a face on it. Push two ends of a pipe cleaner through the caterpillar's head for antennae, and push a sequin on each tip of the wire. Print your name on the caterpillar's head.

Whenever friends come to visit you or you go to visit them, have each friend sign his name on a circle. You can glue each circle onto your caterpillar. When you visit your doctor, the fire station, police station, or the person who works on your car, you might ask them to add their names to your caterpillar of friends, too.

Thoughtful Treasure Hunt (early elementary)

When your mother isn't around, make a treasure hunt for her in the kitchen. Hide little surprises in unexpected places. You can bury a pretty picture of a flower with a poem about flowers on it in the bottom of the canister of flour. Hide a note somewhere on the refrigerator, promising to clean the fridge for her. Fold up a paper with a Bible verse about honey, and tape it on the honey jar.

You can make treasure hunts for other members of your family, too. Wrap a small present and hide it under a brother's or sister's pillow. Write coupons good for several car washes to be performed by yourself, and hide them in your dad's sock drawer. You can think of many more ideas yourself that will keep your family smiling at unexpected times, in unexpected places.

Letter Writing (later elementary)

Is there anyone you haven't seen for a long time who would enjoy a letter from you? It could be a teacher from a school you used to attend, a neighbor who has moved to a different part of town, or a cousin you rarely get to see.

You can make letter writing

extra fun by making your letters a little different. Write on a postcard, and cut it up in several large pieces. Then mail your letter puzzle in an envelope. Cut your letter in half, and mail half one day, and the other half the next. Write a letter in code, and send the code first.

You can also write a letter cartoon-style. Clip cartoon characters out of the newspaper, and cut out the words. Use your own words in the balloons, letting the cartoon characters pass on your news and other comments to your friend.

Julie and Joy were best friends. They went everywhere together, talked by the hour, and kept each other's secrets.

Maybe you didn't know that friends come with a price tag. Of course they don't really, but keeping a friend does cost you some effort, for your friend deserves your loyalty. That means, as Julie learned, putting your friend's best interests above your own wishes.

Uncle Arthur

The Price of Friendship

Julie and Joy were each 9 years old, and the best of friends. They went everywhere together, talked by the hour, and kept each other's secrets.

One beautiful summer afternoon Joy said she would like to go to the beach.

"Fine," answered Julie. "When shall we meet?"

"How about three o'clock?" asked Joy.

"Three o'clock it is," said Julie. "I'll meet you at the usual place."

Less than an hour later Uncle Jack arrived. He had been overseas for a long time and had just returned. He was full of good spirits and eager to take the whole family out for a big picnic in the park.

"When?" asked Julie.

"Today, of course," said Uncle Jack. "This very afternoon."

91

Should she keep her promise to go with Joy? Or should she forget her and go with the rest of the family?

Now Julie faced a real problem. She tried to phone Joy to tell her about Uncle Jack's picnic. Perhaps she could make different plans for going to the beach. But Julie couldn't reach Joy. Should she keep her promise to go with Joy? Or should she forget Joy and go with the rest of the family?

What should she do? She decided to ask Mother about it. Mother always had good advice.

"You made a promise to Joy," Mother said, "and you should stand by it. That is the price of friendship. Never let your friends down if you want to keep them."

"But Mama," said Julie, "wouldn't it be all right just once? After all, Uncle Jack doesn't come very often, and I'd love to go to the family picnic."

"No," said Mother. "Not even once. Joy is your extraspecial friend, so be loyal to her. Always."

"But Joy wouldn't do it for me," said Julie.

"How do you know?" asked Mother. "Anyway, we shouldn't lower our own standards because of what other people do. When you make a promise you should keep it, no matter if something more attractive turns up."

Julie thought it all over and decided to take Mother's advice. She met Joy on time at the usual place. They played on the beach awhile, talking and laughing as only little girls can.

Suddenly Julie had an idea. "Let's go home and change our clothes and go for a walk," she cried. Joy agreed.

It wasn't long before they found themselves opposite the park gates.

"Let's go in," said Julie. "Uncle Jack's picnic may still be going on."

It was! And what a wonderful welcome Uncle Jack gave them both. He said he was proud of them for being so loyal to each other. "Loyalty," he said, just as Mother had said before, "is the price of friendship."

Then he piled ice cream in their dishes right up to the top, as if to say, "This is how much I think of you."

You can have a successful STORYTIME™ adventure by simply reading the story to your child. The activities below are optional additions to your adventure. Use an activity after the story is read, or save it for later. The grade levels may guide your choice, but select the activity your child will most enjoy.

Discussing the Story

A friend is a special treasure that deserves to be taken care of. Many new items that you buy in a store come with instructions on how to care for them. If you were to write a "care tag" that would give instructions on how to care for a friend, what would you say?

Try making one with your friend's name on it, and hang it somewhere in your room to remind you of the kinds of things you should do to keep your friend happy.

Fun Footnotes

Abraham Lincoln had a deep respect for people of all ages and in all stations of life.

During the Civil War, he did not think of the Southerners as enemies that should be exterminated. He felt they were erring human beings. When a lady rebuked him for thinking kindly of his enemies instead of wanting to destroy them, Lincoln replied, "Why, madam, do I not destroy my enemies when I make them my friends?"

STORYTIME Fun Activities

Books Are Friends (preschool)

There is a verse about books that goes like this:

Books Are Friends

Books are keys to wisdom's treasure;
Books are gates to lands of pleasure;
Books are paths that upward lead;
Books are friends. Come, let us read.
—Emilie Poulsson

As you read more and more books, some become your favorites. You read them again and again, like an old friend. Sometimes your favorites change, and you will probably always be making new friends. But it's good to keep your old friends, too, even when your old friend is a book.

Look over your books, or the books in the library where you go. Is there one that is really a favorite? Draw a picture, or make something out of clay that reminds you of your special book. At the bottom of the picture, or on the base of the clay, write "My friend, _____ (name of the book)." Then write a sentence about why the book is your friend.

Music Is a Friend (early elementary)

The best way to make friends with a musical instrument is to find one you'd like to play, and learn how to play it. Most instruments are rather expensive, but you can check pawn shops for some good buys.

You can also make many instruments. To make a drum, stretch a piece of rubber inner tube tightly over a hollow frame such as a wooden box or a barrel and tack it down. If you press your hand down on the edge of stretched rubber, you can change the pitch.

To make a set of pan pipes, cut half-inch plastic pipe (PVC) into graduated lengths. Sand the ends of the pipes, and fit each one with a cap. (Both PVC pipe and caps are available at hardware stores.) To tune the pipes, lengthen the pipe by adjusting the caps, or shorten the pipe by filing or sanding the top of the pipe. Tape the pipes together.

To play the pipes, put your lips at the edge of a pipe. Draw your lips tight in a half-smile, and blow softly down and across the pipe.

Finding Friends in Art (later elementary)

It's fun to make your own artwork. You will also enjoy looking at the artwork of other people. Since everybody is different, you will probably have your own ideas of the kinds of artwork you enjoy. You may like the clean, simple lines of Japanese paintings and prints. You might enjoy the play of light in the impressionist paintings such as Monet and Renoir.

Picasso used color and shapes to express many different kinds of ideas. Van Gogh has a lot of energy and electricity in his paintings. Remington's artwork describes much of the drama and excitement of the early West. Gauguin loved to paint happy, peaceful scenes of the South Pacific in exotic, yet harmonious colors.

As you study different artists and their work, you will become friends with them through their paintings. You will understand what you like in the world around you better. You can write to Publications Service, National Gallery of Art, Washington, D.C. 20565 for a catalog of inexpensive 11" x 14" art posters to hang in your room.

As the boys rolled on the ground, Mother called from the window.

Have you ever applied for the position of peacemaker in your home? Anyone can do the job, young or old; you just need to be willing to be first in offering to help work out a happy solution to a problem between two people. Even if one of them is you!

Uncle Arthur

Love Conquers All

What a noise was coming from the backyard! You've never heard anything like it—at least I hope you never have.

Bert and Bob had been playing Indians around the little summer house at the end of the lawn. Bob was dressed up as a chief with feathers he had saved from the chicken house. Bert was supposed to be the White man trying to keep the Indian out of the summer house.

Then the quarrel began. Bob said that Bert was dead, because he had shot him with his bow and arrow. Bert said that he wasn't dead, and wasn't going to be dead for Bob or anybody else.

"You're a cheat," cried Bob; "you are dead!"

"I'm not a cheat, and I'm not dead," cried Bert.

"You are."

"I'm not."

"Don't play then; play by yourself."

Both boys got more and more angry, and all of a sudden Bob hit Bert on the nose. There was a tussle, and then the boys heard a voice coming from the dining room window.

"Come in, come in, both of you," cried Mother. "I won't have this noise in the yard. What will the neighbors think of you?"

Silently the two boys walked toward the house.

"It was his fault," said Bert.

"Wasn't; it was Bert's," said Bob.

"Never mind; come along, both of you, and sit on these two chairs. And not a sound from either of you for the next quarter of an hour."

Bob and Bert sat down at opposite sides of the room and glared at each other in silence. When Mother said they were not to talk, she meant it.

Very slowly the minutes ticked away. The boys thought they had never before sat so still for so long. Just before the quarter of an hour was up, Mother came into the room again.

"I'm going to tell you a little story," she said. Their faces brightened.

"Many years ago," began Mother, "Indians used to roam over the wide plains and forests of North America. There were terrible fights between the Indians and the White people who were trying to settle in America. Naturally, the Indians felt that the country belonged to them and that the White people had no right to it. They fought to keep what was theirs. Many of the White people were very cruel, and this only made matters worse.

"One day a man landed in America, determined to try a different method with the Indians. His name was William Penn. He thought he would try to make

*William Penn determined to make friends with the Indians. The peo-
ple laughed, saying he would be tomahawked and scalped in no time.*

friends with the Indians instead of fighting them. But
his own people laughed at him. They said that he
would be tomahawked and scalped in no time."

"Didn't he take a gun with him?" asked Bert.

"Your silence period isn't up yet," said Mother.

"Oh," muttered Bert, getting quiet again.

"No, he didn't take a gun with him," Mother went
on. "Soon after he arrived in the new country he
called all the Indians together. They came in large
numbers, in all their war paint, and carrying their
weapons. Probably they suspected a trap. Penn and
his friends were all unarmed. Penn talked to them as
no White man had ever spoken to them before.

"'We must use no weapons against our fellow
creatures,' he said. 'Good faith and goodwill toward
man are our defenses. We believe you will deal kindly
and justly by us. And we will deal kindly and justly by
you. We meet on the broad highway of faith and

101

goodwill. No advantage shall be taken on either side, but all shall be openness and love, for we are all one flesh and blood.'

"After he had finished speaking, Penn pulled a piece of paper out of his pocket. On the paper he had  drawn up a treaty to be signed by the Indians and himself. He read it over to them, while they listened with astonishment. This is how part of the agreement read:

"'We will be brethren, my people and your people, as the children of one Father. All the paths shall be open to the Christian and the Indian. The doors of the Christian shall be open to the Indian, and the wigwams of the Indian shall be open to the Christian.'

"Most of the White people who heard about the treaty said Penn was foolish. The Indian chiefs agreed to the treaty, however, gave Penn a pledge of good faith, and went away content.

"Time went on. In other parts of America there was constant fighting. But in Pennsylvania, which was named after Penn, there was peace. When Penn wanted land from the Indians, he bought it. He insisted that if a White man injured an Indian, he must be punished just the same as if he had injured a White man. He said that the White people must not sell bad goods to the Indians when trading with them. Everybody had to be fair."

"Wasn't he ever scalped?" asked Bob, with one eye on the clock.

"No, indeed," said Mother. "The Indians loved him

too much for that. For many years no unarmed man was killed in Pennsylvania. You see, by treating the Indians kindly, Penn won their friendship and kept peace. It's too bad that the Whites in general didn't follow his example."

Bob and Bert were fast cooling down now.

"I suppose I should make peace with that Indian over there," said Bert, pointing at Bob.

"It would certainly be a very nice thing to do," said Mother.

"Time's up," cried Bob, looking at the clock again. With happy smiles, Bert and Bob slid off their chairs and ran out into the yard.

You can have a successful STORYTIME™ adventure by simply reading the story to your child. The activities below are optional additions to your adventure. Use an activity after the story is read, or save it for later. The grade levels may guide your choice, but select the activity your child will most enjoy.

Discussing the Story

Using force such as fighting or arguing rarely ever solves a problem; it usually makes things worse. Talking is one of the best ways of solving problems. If you have a problem with someone else, talking to that person often helps both of you understand what to do.

Which statement sounds like the best way to discuss a problem? Why?

"You always make me late. Why can't you quit fooling around and hurry up?"

"It looks like we're going to be late again. Can I help you do anything? We need to figure out what to do so we aren't always late."

Fun Footnotes

William Penn was a Quaker. King Charles II owed Penn's father a debt, which Penn asked him to pay with wilderness land in America. The land was called Pennsylvania, meaning Penn's woods, and became a refuge for persecuted Quakers. The Frame of Government that Penn drew up for his colony contained such sound principles of government that it influenced many later charters, including the Constitution of the United States.

STORYTIME Fun Activities

Three Little Indians (preschool)

Indians depended on their skills to move quietly and quickly through the woods to survive. This is an action poem. You will need to make three little Indian faces out of paper. Put a different colored feather in each Indian's hair, and tape a band (paper or pipe cleaner) on the back of the faces, so they will stay on your fingers.

Three little Indians (hold up three Indian faces on right hand)

Hiding in the trees (faces peek from behind fingers of left hand)

Tiptoeing lightly (bend slightly, and tiptoe)

Through rustling leaves.

Here is a stream to cross

With a quick dash;

One jumps across—good! (hold up one Indian, and jump)

Two jumps across—good! (hold up two Indians, and jump)

Three jumps across—oh, no! (hold up three Indians)

SPLASH! (fall)

Hornbook (early elementary)

Paper used to be so expensive that very few people could afford books. The paper that children's first lessons were printed on was pasted on a piece of board with a handle. Often the handle had a hole in it so it could hang on a cord from around a child's neck. The Colonists covered the expensive paper with horn to protect it.

You can make a hornbook. On a piece of paper, write out the alphabet in uppercase and lowercase letters, the numerals, and the Lord's Prayer.

With your parents' help, use a coping saw to cut out a ¼-inch hardboard or plywood board with a handle. Drill a hole in the handle and glue this paper on it. Spray the paper with acrylic. You might also want to use a glazing compound (available at a hardware store) to protect the front and back of the board.

Obstacle Course (later elementary)

Indians played many ball games and guessing games. They enjoyed races and other games that tested their skills in throwing, agility, and strength.

You can have fun testing your strength and agility by building an obstacle course. Your obstacle course can include things to wiggle under, climb over, struggle through, or swing on. You can run through a set of tires laid in two rows, run across a log, or use a rope to swing across a ditch or down a hill. Suspend a stout stick on two ropes to climb over.

An inside obstacle course can include squeezing between a chair and a wall, crawling under a bed, running through a hall full of balloons, jumping over a rope, and crossing a set of "stepping-stones" (pieces of carpet or linoleum) set at awkward angles and distances.

As a variation, run the obstacle course in teams. Time each team, and set penalties for running the course incorrectly (bursting a balloon or falling off a "stepping-stone" or log, for example).

Don't forget to ask an adult to check your course for safety.

Frank trudged to school greatly worried. What could he do now?

The best present you can give always includes some part of yourself. The boy in this story used a very simple way to show his mother how much she meant to him. Read the story, and see how well it worked!

Uncle Arthur

Mother's Present

F rank was very much puzzled. Two birthdays were coming along soon in his home, and he just didn't know what to do about them. Like most little boys, he was very low on funds. To buy two presents seemed quite impossible.

Frank decided to speak to Mother about it, even though one of the birthdays was hers. Anyhow, he thought, Mother always understood. Perhaps he would get an idea of what to do while they were talking.

He was pleased when Mother herself brought up the subject.

"Frank, dear," she said one afternoon, "you won't forget Uncle Herbert's birthday, will you?"

"No," said Frank, "I won't forget Uncle Herbert. But," he said, lowering his voice to a whisper, "there's another birthday besides that one, which is more important. Of course, I want to please Uncle Herbert, but

The more Frank thought about it, the more he liked the idea. In between classes he found a corner where he could be alone.

I want to make you happy, too!"

Mother was so touched that she stopped what she was doing. She put her arms around Frank and kissed him—which made Frank forget all about trying to find just what kind of birthday presents he should give.

The days passed. Soon the morning of Mother's birthday dawned. Frank still had not been able to make up his mind about what he should do.

He went off to school greatly worried. What could he do now? Oh, why hadn't he decided before! It suddenly dawned on Frank that he couldn't buy anything that day in any case. The stores would all be closed by the time he could get to the city. He felt ashamed of himself for having left it until too late.

All through his classes Frank could think of nothing else. How could he go home to Mother without a present for her?

Then a bright idea came to him. At least he could

write Mother a letter. She might be glad of that. It would be a different sort of present, anyway.

The more he thought of it, the more he liked the idea. Between classes, Frank found a corner where he could be alone, and there he wrote his birthday letter to Mother.

He told Mother how much he loved her. He said that he wanted to grow up to be a good man. He told her that he'd earn money so he could buy her all the lovely things he would like to buy her now but couldn't. He told her that he would always love and care for her as long as she lived.

When he had finished the letter, Frank sealed it carefully. When he got home, he crept quietly up to the front door and dropped it in the mail box. Then he made a big rat-a-tat like the mailman, and ran quickly away.

When Frank returned, there were tears in Mother's eyes. But what a lovely smile was on her face! Mother said that the letter was the loveliest present Frank could possibly have sent her. She had never had a present she valued so much.

One day four years later, I met this mother on a train. She told me the story, and added, "That letter is the most precious treasure I possess."

Perhaps your mother would like to have a birthday present like this someday from you. Why not plan to write it now?

111

❖ Exploring the Story ❖

You can have a successful STORYTIME™ adventure by simply reading the story to your child. The activities below are optional additions to your adventure. Use an activity after the story is read, or save it for later. The grade levels may guide your choice, but select the activity your child will most enjoy.

Discussing the Story

This might come as a surprise to you. Did you know that it isn't easy being a mother? Watch yours closely. You'll probably see a very busy lady who has many different jobs to do. Sometimes you might be able to tell that she worries a little about whether she is doing a good job with all her different duties.

Since you are her child, taking care of you is one of her most important jobs, and she probably is concerned about whether she is doing a good job. Do you know how you can make your mother feel good? Show her how glad you are for all the work she is putting into you! Things you do for her show her she is worth the time and effort it takes you to plan for her happiness. It helps her feel loved.

Fun Footnotes

The American poet William Ross Wallace (1819-1881) wrote *The Hand That Rules the World.* Can you guess whose hand that would be? Read the following poem. Do you agree with the poet?

They say that man is mighty,
He governs land and sea;
He wields a mighty sceptre
O'er lesser powers that be.
But a mightier power and stronger
Man from his throne has hurled,
The hand that rocks the cradle
Is the hand that rules the world.

STORYTIME Fun Activities

Fruit and Vegetable Prints (preschool)

You can design wrapping paper and cards with prints from fruit and vegetables. For a variation, try using colored paper with white or colored tempera paint for making the prints. Cut peppers or oranges in half before dipping them in the paint. Squeeze most of the juice out of the orange half first, but be careful not to break the sections. You can make cross cuts in pieces of celery or carrots to print crescent shapes, circles, or ovals. Try printing a border to frame a picture, or a poem you wrote.

Writing a Poem (early elementary)

Some of the best poems are the ones you write yourself. Writing poems has a curious way of helping you see better! You might want to write about what you like best, what you think about most, or what grabs your attention.

One way to start writing a poem is to put down on a piece of paper all the words and ideas you have about something. Put down words that express feelings. Put down words that make pictures. After you have put down all the ideas you can, pick the words that make the strongest, clearest picture of what you want to say.

You can experiment with the different sounds the words make, and the different beats the words make together. Experiment with the way words look on the page. Make them go up or down, or put them in a shape like a tree, a bell, an arrow, or an exclamation point. You can make words sing a song in someone else's heart.

Making Dyes With Natural Materials (later elementary)

It's fun to experiment with the natural dyes in the plants that grow around you. You can dye turkey feathers if they are available (wash these first with soap and water), or pieces of white cotton. Make designs on the cotton by painting it first with melted wax, dyeing it, and then ironing the material between several layers of paper towels to remove the wax. (Get your mom to help you with the iron.) This is a technique used in batik, a famous Indonesian art.

You can also tie the material in bunches with rubber bands before you dye it. This is called tie dyeing.

Use a piece of dyed material for a handkerchief,
a card, or a pin cushion for your mother.

You will get the best results from your dyeing
experiments if you boil the plant materials until you
have extracted most of the color. Let the liquid cool,
and strain it through a cloth. Boil the liquid again, and
fix the color with vinegar and salt. Carefully dip
your materials in the hot liquid. You can make dyes
from the following materials, or experiment and find
other dyes.

Yellow:

    Yellow onion skins
    Marigold petals
    Goldenrod stalks and
        flowers

Red:
    Red onion skins
    Cranberries
    Beets
    Dandelion roots

Green:
    Rhubarb leaves
    Spinach leaves

Blue:
    Blackberries
    Sunflower seeds

Brown:
    Sumac leaves
    Hickory bark
    Walnut hulls

PART THREE

THE STORYGUIDE™ SECTION

HOW CHARACTER IS FORMED

What Is Character?

When we speak of character, we refer to one's moral or ethical strength, how one responds to matters of right and wrong. Character is, as Dwight L. Moody so graphically defined it, "what you are in the dark." Our character is not always immediately visible, yet it is revealed in every major decision we make during a lifetime, and in all the habits and attitudes that make us unique individuals.

Why Is Character Development Important to Parents?

Character development is important to parents for one obvious reason: character does not come as a ready-made package. Rather it is formed, shaped, and molded through all the influences and experiences of our lives. Parents occupy the most important place in the development of a child's character, for the beliefs and attitudes held by the parents, the things they consider important, will be largely passed on to the child.

Is Character Formed All at Once?

Sociologists have shown that character is developed in stages. The first stage is a self-centered one. An infant learns to do what is rewarding and to avoid unpleasant experiences. At this point, right and wrong are connected to what feels good and what is uncomfortable.

The second stage of character development centers around conformity. In this stage a child learns to live within the rules of his home. His good behavior may even become a habit. The reasons that make anything right or wrong are not considered. The child, if he thinks about it at all, merely assumes "that's just the way we do things around here."

Parents occupy the most important place in the development of a child's character.

In the third stage of character development, children begin to make some personal decisions about right and wrong. As he exercises his own judgment, a child is building an ethical system of his own. Sometimes his decisions may seem to an adult to be inconsistent, even irrational. That's because his ethical system is incomplete, is still in the process of forming.

We arrive at the fourth stage of character development when we have formed a strong, consistent internal standard of right and wrong. At this point our actions take into consideration the feelings and needs of others. But we choose to do what is right because it is right, not because of what others say or do. For most of us, this degree of character development is the work of a lifetime.

You will quickly recognize that there are many in-between areas in these basic stages, areas in which individuals may have characteristics belonging to more than one stage. A person may also operate in one stage in one area of his life and another stage in a different area.

As you teach your children and help them shape their character, remember these stages of development. Attempt to understand the issues through the eyes of your children. Acceptable, appropriate behavior is possible in each stage, even before the understanding of right and wrong is fully developed.

What's the Best Way I Can Aid My Children in the Development of a Strong Character?

The setting of a positive, consistent example in a caring, nurturing way is the most important thing you as a parent can do to influence strong character development in your children. The lessons you teach by your example do more than all the words of instruction you give.

But don't neglect instruction. Talk to your child in every possible circumstance so he can have the information necessary to make correct decisions on his own. Even the stories you read together play a good part in your contribution to the development of positive character traits.

And your discipline needs to be consistent and caring. The child must always know that you are acting in his best interest. (See the section "Confident Parenting" on pages 122-127 for more discussion on this point.)

What Role Do Spiritual Values Have in Character Development?

Principles that are highly prized and recommended in the Bible, both in its instruction and in the examples it sets forth (such as kindness, love, sharing, truthfulness, service), are valued and appreciated by people all around the world.

Parents who share biblical values with their children are providing an ethical framework of right and wrong. When those values are combined with a parental example consistent with what is being taught, children receive the basic foundation and information necessary for positive character development, a foundation that will help guide their decisions throughout life.

CONFIDENT PARENTING

In the last few decades scientific and technological knowledge has increased by gigantic leaps and bounds. But for all that extra knowledge, no one has designed a child care system better than a loving home. You, as your child's parent, are still the person best qualified to take care of your child! You can feel good about that. You can feel confident.

Discovering the best way to go about bringing up your child takes time, thought, and attention. Parents receive lots of child-rearing advice from well-meaning friends and relatives. You may not wish or know how to adapt all this advice to your specific situation. But in the working of simple principles you will find a comfortable pattern of parenting.

Let's examine a few of those simple principles.

1. Teach Respect by Being Respectful.

Smile at your children. Listen to their chatter and be pleasant as you answer them. Catch their words as if you really need to know what they are saying (you do!). Be courteous. Apologize if you accidentally bump into them. Thank them for their little attentions and achievements as you would thank an honored friend. Defer to their opinions whenever possible. Ask them where they would like to go for a walk, or what they would like to wear. Correct them gently. Treat them the way you want them to treat you and others.

When you have treated your children with respect and dignity, they will respond to your requests with respect and dignity. They will know you have their best interests at heart, and that they can depend on you. Thus respect leads to trust. Respect and trust are the first lessons of childhood. They form the foundation of all the lessons you want your children to learn.

2. Few Character Traits Cause More Joy in the Hearts of Parents Than Obedience.

Obedience gives us confidence that our children won't play in the street. Obedience assists us in teaching our children the habits and values they need. Obedience keeps the stress level low.

But it's also true that few character traits cause as much parental discouragement. Especially when the kids are running away from you in the supermarket, or when grandma glimpses a messy bedroom, or when a little one stretches up to his full height and says, "No!"

Here are a few basic pointers about this vital, yet puzzling, quality.

a. *Don't confuse disobedience with learning.* Many behaviors that seem disobedient are merely the natural workings of a child's growing interest. When your little boy pours cereal and milk from the bowl onto the high chair, he's probably just performing his first chemistry experiment. He's learning how things feel and what they're like when mixed together. Be sure to distinguish between disobedience and childish enthusiasm, between defiance and an inborn desire to learn.

b. *Make it easy to obey.* Do everything you can do to make your instructions simple and easy to follow. Eliminate distractions long enough to assure your directions are carried through. (For example, turn off the TV before you tell a child what you want done. Or tackle cleaning responsibilities in the morning when the child has energy, not when he or she is tired and needs a nap.) Help your child obey by making it easy to obey.

c. *Try to work on one thing at a time.* Sometimes you'll meet with resistance. You may ask your child to do something, and instead of doing it he throws himself on the ground, kicking and screaming. Don't get angry and lecture him for his bad temper. Calmly pick him up and, without referring to the screaming, take him to where he needs to be and make sure that he does what you asked him to do.

d. *Mean what you say.* Don't give orders unless you're prepared to follow through. If you tell your child to pick up his toys, be sure he picks up his toys. Don't walk away and in an hour or so come back with, "I thought I told you . . ." This type of parental behavior teaches a child to disobey.

Help your child obey by making it easy to obey.

A few words about spanking. There may be times when you reach the end of your rope and you think a spanking is necessary. The trouble is that most of us spank our children at the worst possible times, usually when we're angry and a little bit out of control. If you get to the point that spanking seems appropriate, remember these cautions:

● In the majority of instances, other methods of discipline will work better than spanking. By trying these other methods first, you may find your discipline to be effective without spanking.

● Spank only when you are in full emotional control of yourself. One spanking lovingly and sensitively applied can work wonders. Spanking in anger fails as an effective means of discipline.

● Spank only when you can take the time to do it right. Talk about it before you do it. Be sure your facts are straight. Be confident your child understands why this is about to happen. Talk about it afterward. Tell your child you punished him because you love him. Talk about how you hope you never have to do it again. Mix lots of hugs with your talking. And don't be afraid to cry together. Your loving attitude is as important as the spanking itself.

3. As Your Child's Abilities Develop, He Will Need to Learn to Carry More Responsibilities.

The more completely the early lessons of respect and obedience have been learned, the easier other lessons of life will come. As your child's abilities develop, he will need to learn to carry more and more responsibilities But even preschoolers and children in the early elementary years respond positively when asked to help. Keep their chores easy at first and increase their responsibility as you see they can handle it. Of course, you'll want to remember that you're dealing with children. Don't make them work all day long at tasks that make even you tired. When their chores are done, let them play a favorite game, or go outside, or, better yet, spend some extra time with you.

Remember, too, how much easier it is to enjoy fulfilling our responsibilities when our efforts are appreciated. Be quick to thank your child. In your child's hearing, tell others what a big help he or she is. Point out his successes much more often than his failures.

4. Pay Attention to Your Child's Friendships.

As your child becomes older, he will depend more and more on others' opinions to guide his behavior. Invite his friends over often. Make them feel welcome. Join in some of their games and activities, and listen to their conversations. Your child may need your guidance in choosing good friends.

The lessons in obedience and relationships your child learns early in life will also help him relate better to authority figures outside the home, such as teachers, principals, police.

5. Give Your Child All the Information He Needs to Make Independent Judgments.

As your child's reasoning powers develop, use more explanations, demonstrations, and illustrations in your conversations. Little by little, allow your child to make decisions. Begin with small things. Structure the decision so that either choice will be pleasing to you ("Would you like to wear this dress today or this one?" "Would you like to start your meal with your salad? or Would you rather eat your salad at the same time you're eating everything else?"). When your child makes a good decision on his own, be sure to talk about it. Say things such as, "You're really getting good at making decisions." Or, "Your decision made a lot of sense to me. I'm so proud of you."

And in those inevitable times when the wrong decision is made, allow your child to see the consequences. Discuss the options with him and help him understand what went wrong.

The earlier and more completely these lessons are learned, the easier will be your role as parent. And you will find, as all good teachers do, that before long you've worked yourself right out of a job. Your child will have become a mature, responsible, loving adult, one with whom your friendship testifies to the success of your methods of confident parenting.